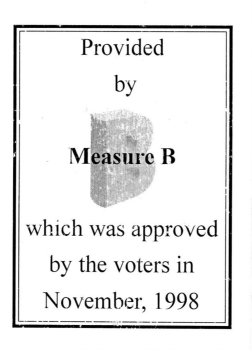

Provided

by

Measure B

which was approved

by the voters in

November, 1998

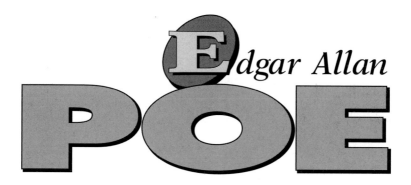

Biography.

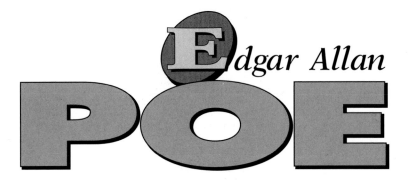

Edgar Allan POE

Tom Streissguth

Lerner Publications Company
Minneapolis

*To Christine and family, for a poetic
surprise—August 5, 2000*

A&E and **BIOGRAPHY** are trademarks of the A&E Television Networks,
registered in the United States and other countries.

Some of the people profiled in this series have also been featured in
A&E's acclaimed BIOGRAPHY series, which is available on videocassette
from A&E Home Video. Call 1-800-423-1212 to order.

Lerner Publications Company
A division of Lerner Publishing Group
241 First Avenue North
Minneapolis, MN 55401 U.S.A.

Website address: www.lernerbooks.com

Library of Congress Cataloging-in-Publication Data

Streissguth, Thomas, 1958–
    Edgar Allan Poe / by Tom Streissguth.
      p.   cm. — (A&E biography)
    Includes bibliographical references and index.
    Summary: Presents the life of the nineteenth-century American author
famous for his detective stories, horror stories, and poetry.
    ISBN 0-8225-4991-3 (lib.bdg. : alk. paper)
    1. Poe, Edgar Allan, 1809–1849—Juvenile literature. 2. Authors,
American—19th century—Biography—Juvenile literature. [1. Poe,
Edgar Allan, 1809–1849. 2. Authors, American.] I. Title. II. Series.
PS2631 .S86   2001
818'.309—dc21   00-008908

Manufactured in the United States of America
1 2 3 4 5 6 – JR – 06 05 04 03 02 01

CONTENTS

Edgar Allan Poe's life changed forever after the death of his mother, actress Eliza Poe, above, *when he was only two years old.*

Chapter **ONE**

ORPHANED

EDGAR ALLAN POE'S STORY "THE BLACK CAT" appeared on August 19, 1843, in the *United States Saturday Post*. It read:

> No sooner had the reverberation of my blows sunk into silence than I was answered by a voice from within the tomb! —by a cry, at first muffled and broken, like the sobbing of a child, and then quickly swelling into one long, loud, and continuous scream . . . a wailing shriek, half of horror and half of triumph, such as might have arisen only out of hell. . . . Swooning, I staggered to the opposite wall. For one instant the party upon the stairs remained motionless, through extremity of

terror and of awe. In the next, a dozen stout arms were tolling at the wall. . . . The corpse, already greatly decayed and clotted with gore, stood erect before the eyes of the spectators. Upon its head . . . sat the [cat] whose craft had seduced me into murder.

The thirty-four-year-old author lived in poverty in a modest house in Philadelphia, Pennsylvania. Urged on by his fears, his ambition, and his vivid imagination, Edgar had written many stories such as "The Black Cat." In all his works, he sought to create a certain effect—wonderment, fear, beauty, horror—that would send chills down the spines of his readers.

Edgar had experienced his share of fearful and unhappy moments. It had been more than thirty years since the most miserable day of his life: December 8, 1811. On that day, two-year-old Edgar had watched his mother, actress Eliza Poe, lie still and quiet in a boardinghouse in Richmond, Virginia. Too ill to raise her head, Eliza had struggled to speak her last words. That day, the curtain fell on the brief life of Eliza Poe, leaving her children to make their way in the world as orphans.

ARRIVING IN AMERICA

Eliza Arnold arrived in America from England in 1795, when she was eight years old. Her stage career began on April 15, 1796, in Boston. After this debut, she played lovesick women, naive country girls, and tough scamps from the big city. She could sing and dance and memorize long, difficult speaking parts. She played in the cities of Newport, Rhode Island, and Charleston, South Carolina, as well as in Boston and New York. In all of these cities, the critics praised her acting. Her long, dark hair, large and expressive eyes, and soft voice brought her the attention and applause of the public.

In Alexandria, Virginia, Eliza married a young actor named Charles Hopkins. But on October 26, 1805, Hopkins died of yellow fever. Eliza then met David Poe, a gentleman from Baltimore, Maryland. David Poe had left a promising career as a lawyer to become an actor. But his stage fright and awkward speaking manner often drew hisses from audiences and ridicule from critics.

In the first week of April 1806, Eliza married David Poe. Life was hard and money was very short for Mr. and Mrs. Poe. Their theater company staged many performances as benefits, using the money they earned to save the struggling Poes from starvation. The Poes, nevertheless, had started a family. On January 30, 1807, Eliza gave birth to William Henry. Unable to earn enough money to care for the infant, the couple made the devastating decision to give custody of their son to David Poe's parents, who were better off. On January 19, 1809, Edgar Poe was born.

THE FAMILY OF POES

Desperately poor, David Poe begged for a few dollars from a wealthy cousin, George Poe, of Stockerton, Pennsylvania. George thought his cousin was a worthless scoundrel and told him that he never wished to hear from him again. After this blow and arguments with Eliza, David Poe disappeared. Eliza continued to act in New York, then Norfolk, VA, then Richmond. Sympathetic friends and audiences gave her charity, offering her some relief from her poverty and abandonment.

During the following months, Eliza slowly lost her health. She came down with tuberculosis, a contagious lung disease that was very hard to cure. On December 20, 1810, she gave birth to Rosalie. Several ladies of Richmond helped Eliza in her last months. One of them, Frances "Fanny" Allan, was the wife of the Richmond merchant John Allan. The Allans had enjoyed many of Eliza's performances. Now Fanny wanted to help the actress who had entertained her so well. She brought warm clothing, food, and medicine to Eliza's sickroom.

In the fall of 1811, a gentleman from Richmond, Samuel Mordecai, visited Eliza. He wrote the following letter to his sister:

> A singular fashion prevails here this season—it is—charity. Mrs. Poe, who you know is a very handsome woman, happens to be very sick, and

(having quarreled and parted with her husband) is destitute. The most fashionable place of resort, now is—her chamber—And the skill of cooks and nurses is exerted to procure her delicacies. Several other sick persons also receive a portion of these fashionable visits and delicacies—It is a very laudable fashion and I wish it may last long.

Even with all the charity she received, Eliza could not overcome her illness. That December, Edgar, William Henry, and Rosalie gathered in their mother's room to hear her last words and witness her quiet death.

John Allan, above, *became Edgar's foster father after Eliza Poe's death.*

Chapter TWO

A DISTANT FATHER

AFTER ELIZA'S DEATH, FANNY ALLAN, ONE OF THE women who had helped Eliza in her last months, wrote to David Poe's parents in Baltimore. She offered to take Edgar, see to his care and upbringing, and give him an education. Another wealthy Richmond family offered to care for Rosalie. The Poe family agreed.

Edgar had started his life in crowded rooms and drafty theaters. After his mother died, he moved to the Allans' big, warm house in Richmond. He had books to read, a yard to play in, and a room of his own. The Allans also took trips in horse-drawn carriages out of Richmond to visit the beautiful Shenandoah Valley and the Blue Ridge Mountains in western Virginia.

Frances (Fanny) Allan

But John Allan had little time to spend with his foster son. Instead, Allan spent his days and evenings in his offices, looking after his dealings in tobacco, leather, wine, food, and land. The War of 1812 against Great Britain had hurt Allan's international business, but by this time, the United States was again trading freely with countries across the Atlantic Ocean. Allan was too busy arranging purchases, sales, and shipments to devote much of his time to a frail young boy who was not even related to him.

MOVING TO LONDON

In 1815, John Allan opened an office in London,

where the family moved and rented a house. He sent Edgar to a small boarding school. Two years later, he sent Edgar to the Manor House in Stoke Newington, England, a school run by the Reverend John Bransby. At Manor House, Edgar went by the name of Edgar Allan. Eight years old, he was thin as a razor but still strong enough to walk for miles among the old cottages and ancient hedges near Manor House.

John Allan paid the fees for room, board, tuition, washing, books, shoes, and dancing lessons. He provided Edgar with the best education possible. Allan's homes always held many books, which were expensive and rare items for most families of the time. He wrote Edgar many letters instructing him to study hard and to stay out of mischief. The Rev. Bransby's students learned foreign languages, poetry, mathematics, and religion. Edgar did well at his studies, spending long hours at the desk in his room.

Although Edgar was usually outgoing and friendly, he sometimes fell into a miserable, homesick depression. John Allan stayed in London, attending to business, and Fanny Allan paid little attention to Edgar. To relieve his loneliness and his dark thoughts, Edgar turned to his books of tales and poetry and to the verse of George Gordon Byron, or Lord Byron. In Byron's works, brave men overcame danger with a noble spirit, a stout heart, and a disregard for death.

Edgar also discovered the German poet Johann Wolfgang von Goethe and the English poets Percy

Shelley and William Wordsworth. These poets explored the wide range of human emotions: love, fear, courage, nostalgia, and admiration for natural beauty. They were part of the Romantic movement of writers who rejected the cold reason and strict logic popular in the 1700s.

TROUBLE IN RICHMOND

John Allan's business in London thrived until 1819. In that year, the market for American tobacco collapsed. Unable to sell his goods in Europe, Allan nearly went bankrupt. In 1820, after five years in England, the family again crossed the North Atlantic. This time, John Allan had only a few English pounds in his pocket. His family was poor and its future uncertain.

In Richmond, John Allan moved his family from one lodging to another while he tried to settle his many debts. The Allans lived with John's business partner for a time, and later moved into a small house in a busy neighborhood of tobacco warehouses. Edgar studied in small schools run by tutors and professors. He excelled in the study of ancient Roman poets and learned to read many of their works in Latin.

Gradually, Allan recovered from his business troubles. Then, in 1825, he inherited the enormous sum of $750,000 in money and land from his uncle, William Galt. John Allan became one of the wealthiest men in Richmond, respected and envied by those who knew of him.

Edgar's hometown of Richmond, Virginia, in the 1800s

His business also thrived. The merchants of Richmond were profiting from a time of peace and prosperity in the United States. There were no more wars with Great Britain, and bitter rivalries among different political parties in Washington, D.C., faded into the past. Manufacturing allowed new businesses to flourish, and the country was expanding westward. Later historians would call this time the Era of Good Feelings.

AT THE UNIVERSITY OF VIRGINIA

Edgar paid little attention to his foster father's money or his business. The boy still suffered from loneliness and a feeling that he was unwanted. By this time, Edgar was using "Allan" as his middle name—John Allan had never legally adopted him. Edgar realized that many people did not consider him a legitimate part of the family. He felt awkward and embarrassed by this uncertain status. He grew quiet and sullen, and he began to withdraw from John and Fanny Allan.

Edgar still felt eager to study and learn. He could read Latin and French easily and enjoyed the works of literary masters such as the French playwright Molière. He dreamed of writing poetry as good as that of Lord Byron and other famous English poets. He spent evenings at a small writing desk in his room, weaving stories in verse. He also wrote satires that made fun of familiar Richmond characters—especially the merchants who reminded him of his foster father. At one point, he had written enough plays and poems to gather into a book, which he asked John Allan to help him publish at a local printer. Allan refused, not wanting Edgar to develop an improper pride at seeing his own name in print.

In school, Edgar was ambitious and competitive. He excelled at reading and writing in foreign languages. His slender but athletic body allowed him to shine at sporting activities. He could run quickly, box skillfully, and swim the choppy and dangerous waters of the James River. He loved to overcome challenges and show off for onlookers. He also felt a strong admiration for military life. When he was fifteen, Edgar volunteered for the Junior Morgan Riflemen, an organization for young Richmond boys. He proudly wore the Riflemen's uniform and took command of parade and drill marching whenever he had the chance.

In the fall of 1825, Edgar's brother, William Henry Poe, came from Baltimore to visit him. Together they visited their sister, Rosalie, who was showing signs of developmental disabilities.

That same fall, Edgar met and quickly fell in love with a Richmond girl, Sarah Elmira Royster. The two began to talk of an engagement.

In February 1826, John Allan sent Edgar to the University of Virginia in Charlottesville. According to Allan, a university education would provide Edgar with a good start to a life as an upstanding citizen— probably as a businessman. In turn, Allan would look like a generous foster father. Allan gave Edgar a bit of spending money and stern warnings to study hard.

Edgar attended the University of Virginia, below, *in Charlottesville.*

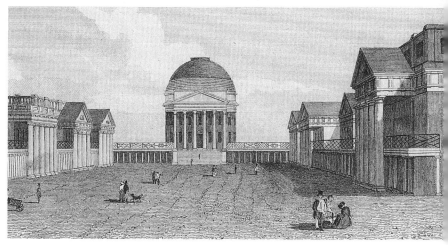

Edgar studied English poetry and began writing his own poems at this desk in his sparsely furnished dormitory room at the University of Virginia.

At the university, Edgar read the works of French and Italian writers and earned praise for translating Latin poetry. The poetry of Lord Byron, Percy Shelley, and others filled his evening hours and inspired him to write more verse. He recited his poems for his classmates, who admired his great skill in turning out playful or tragic verses on whatever subject or theme they suggested.

But his writing earned him nothing, and Edgar could not possibly pay for the many necessities of student life with the money John Allan had given him. The seventeen-year-old quickly ran into serious debt for his clothing and his books. Edgar also made friends who enjoyed gambling at cards. Edgar played and gambled eagerly, and usually lost. He had to borrow money from classmates to make up his debts.

Edgar soon discovered that life at the university was not all peaceful study and good times with friends. There were fights and beatings, vandalism and riots. The students often cheated on their examinations, and many of them became roaring drunk at night. They threatened and sometimes attacked their professors.

Edgar also felt abandoned. Sarah Royster was not answering any of his letters. Edgar wrote often to her from his lonely room, but Sarah remained silent. She was still young—only fifteen years old—and her stern father opposed her engagement to Edgar. Edgar did not know that he was destroying Edgar's letters before they could reach his daughter's eyes and heart.

Edgar returned to Richmond after one year at the university. John Allan refused to lend him any more money for his education. He would not allow Edgar to harm himself and his family's reputation with gambling, drinking, and money trouble.

Leaving Home

Although he admired good writing, John Allan would not support Edgar's dream to be a poet. Allan believed Edgar needed discipline, and a practical routine to settle him down. He wanted Edgar to go into business.

Edgar agreed to work in John Allan's office. But Edgar knew before he started that he wasn't made for the routines of business. His business was poetry; the exploration of feelings and beauty in words. A bitterness grew between Edgar and John Allan that finally reached its stormy climax in an argument on the morning of March 19, 1827. Edgar was irresponsible, said his foster father. He was arrogant and wasteful, self-centered, idle, and demanding. Allan was self-righteous and cold, replied Edgar. He was cheap and did not feel any love or sympathy for his family.)

After the long and angry talk, Edgar stormed away. Without a final word or even a look back, Edgar walked across the porch, down the steps, and into the streets of Richmond. He carried nothing but the clothes on his back.

From a table in the Court House Tavern in central Richmond, Edgar wrote a letter to John Allan. He knew he would never win John Allan's affection, but this letter would mark an important start to a new and better life. He believed that he was now beginning his life in the real world, where the public would reward his talent not with spite and indifference, but with well-deserved glory and fame.

> After my treatment of yesterday and what passed between us this morning, I can hardly think you will be surprised at the contents of this letter. My determination is at length taken—to leave your house and endeavor to find some place in this wide world, where I will be treated—not as you have treated me. . . . Send my trunk etc. to the Court-house Tavern, send me I entreat you some money immediately—as I am in the greatest necessity—if you fail to comply with my request—I tremble for the consequence.
>
> Yours etc.
>
> Edgar A Poe

John Allan was right about one thing, however. Edgar was a very stubborn young man. He would not compromise or give in, and he would live the way he wanted. Nobody would change his mind. John Allan replied to Edgar's pleading letters with silence. He sent no money, nor did he deliver Edgar's trunk of clothes. From this time forward, his foster son would be on his own.

Edgar moved to Boston, Massachusetts, above, *in April 1827.*

Chapter **THREE**

SOLDIER AND CADET

EDGAR DECIDED TO ABANDON RICHMOND AND MOVE to Boston, where he spent many lonely months. He could not find work or sell the poetry he had written. He lived on the very little money he could borrow from friends and people that he met in the streets.

Edgar felt ashamed of his miserable existence. He created stories about himself and adopted a new name—Henri le Rennert. He spread tales of his adventures in Russia, his explorations on the high seas, and his dangerous fighting against the Turks in the mountains of Greece. In May 1827, he turned himself into a real soldier, a career certain to hold adventure. He enlisted in the U.S. Army, where he would have a comfortable bed and steady meals.

Edgar was frail from many months of hunger and poverty. But he had a direct gaze and an air of self-assurance. The army recruiters accepted him. He gave his name as Edgar Perry and his age as twenty-two (he was actually eighteen). The army assigned him to the First Artillery Regiment at Fort Independence, on Boston Harbor.

Military service did not stop Edgar from writing poetry or from trying to publish his works. It was only at the writing table that Edgar could express himself, giving his tangled feelings of loneliness and abandonment a clear voice. He still looked to Byron and Shelley as his models, but he began to develop his own style. In his writing, he explored the border between reality and dreams. The power of the imagination to reshape the often boring real world fascinated him. He wanted the words and the lines he wrote to have a powerful effect on his readers. Edgar saw himself as a literary hypnotist, skillfully commanding emotions to come and go with his poetry.

Not long after Edgar enlisted in the army, a small booklet titled *Tamerlane and Other Poems* appeared in Boston's bookshops. It gave the author's name as "A Bostonian." In fact, the Bostonian was Edgar. He had given the poems to a young printer named Calvin F. S. Thomas, who had agreed to publish this collection. "Tamerlane," the title poem, tells the story of a great soldier, a descendant of Genghis Khan, a warrior leader of the Mongols. In the poem, Tamerlane looks

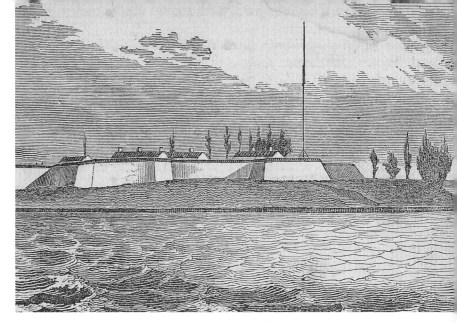

Edgar continued to write poetry while stationed at Fort Independence, above, *Boston.*

back on his life and the terrible sacrifices he has made to realize his ambitions.

SOLDIERING

In the army, Edgar worked hard, followed orders, and stayed out of trouble. His officers noticed his diligence and intelligence. They promoted him to assistant commissary, making him responsible for the regiment's food supplies. On January 1, 1829, Edgar won another promotion, to sergeant major. It was the highest rank he could reach as an enlisted soldier.

Even though he had enlisted for a five-year term, Edgar was ready to leave the army. He believed he had learned enough obedience and self-discipline to last him a lifetime. And the army didn't need him—it was peacetime, and the United States hadn't been in a war since the fight with England in 1812.

Edgar applied to Colonel William Drayton, an officer as well as a friend. Edgar asked to break his enlistment before his term was finished. Colonel Drayton agreed, on two conditions: Edgar must make up with his foster father, who must give his consent.

Edgar agreed and wrote a letter to John Allan. In the letter, he claimed to be more experienced and more mature. The army couldn't help him any more, and he was ready to make his own way in the world.

John Allan did not answer Edgar's letter. Edgar wrote again and then a third time. He tried a new strategy: he asked Allan to help him enter the military academy at West Point, where he would prepare to become an officer. Edgar saw officer training as more useful than an enlistment as a common soldier. He believed this might finally convince Allan to help him.

Then Edgar heard the news that Fanny Allan had died. He took a leave of absence and returned to John Allan's home. In honor of Fanny's memory, Allan and Edgar put aside their differences. Allan agreed to sponsor Edgar's enrollment at West Point.

On April 15, 1829, the U.S. Army discharged Edgar. For his application to West Point, three officers wrote letters of support to the secretary of war, John H. Eaton. John Allan also asked for help from prominent Virginia citizens. With these recommendations, Edgar won a place on a waiting list of candidates for West Point.

While waiting, Edgar moved to Baltimore. There he

arranged for the publication of another book of poetry, *Al Aaraaf*. The publisher—Carey, Lea, and Carey
of Philadelphia—asked Edgar for the money to print
the book. As payment Edgar would earn only a few
copies of the book. Edgar still had no money, so he
asked for John Allan's help in paying for the publication. John Allan angrily refused. He believed there was
no future in such a life, no matter how dearly Edgar
sought it or how talented he might be.

Edgar managed to arrange publication anyway. That
November, his poetry appeared under the true name
of Edgar A. Poe in a volume titled *Al Aaraaf, Tamerlane, and Minor Poems*. Critics in Boston and Baltimore reviewed the book. Some of the reviews were
positive and some were negative. Still, Edgar had
achieved an important goal: critics, booksellers, and a
few readers finally knew his name.

AT WEST POINT

In the spring of 1830, the U.S. Military Academy at
West Point finally admitted Edgar. That summer, he
and the other cadets lived outdoors on the academy's
grounds. He spent mornings drilling and attending
classes. In the afternoons, he studied and drilled some
more. The exercise and outdoor life brought Edgar
good health, and he grew stronger. He took classes in
mathematics and French, and he wrote poetry when
he found the time.

The officers of West Point carefully scheduled every

At the U.S. Military Academy at West Point, above, *Edgar's time was strictly regimented, but he still wrote poetry in his free time.*

minute of Edgar's day, down to the precise time he would go to bed at night and when he would get up in the morning. The other cadets surrounded him like a big family, like a company of brothers. Edgar enjoyed the discipline, but he also enjoyed breaking the rules. On occasion, the cadets secretly drank, gambled, and dueled. Edgar felt as though he were taking part in a great adventure. For a time, he felt content and at ease.

Then Edgar received the news that John Allan had remarried. Allan's second wife was named Louisa Patterson. The wedding took place on October 5, 1830, in New York City, not far from West Point. John

John Allan's second wife, Louisa Patterson, right, wanted Allan to cut off contact with Edgar.

Allan had not invited his foster son to the wedding. Louisa had known Edgar as a headstrong youth in Richmond, and she disliked him. Shortly after the wedding, Allan wrote a final letter to Edgar, asking that he no longer try to contact him.

The letter threw Edgar into a deep depression. He felt himself cut off from his family and his boyhood in Richmond. He felt alone and unappreciated. He could not see a future for himself, and in some moments he despaired of ever finding his way.

Early in 1831, Edgar made the decision to quit West Point after only a year there. Once again, he had to write to John Allan, who again had to give his consent for Edgar to quit the military. In the letter, Edgar poured out his bitter feelings.

You sent me to W. Point like a beggar. The same difficulties are threatening me as before at Charlottesville—and I must resign . . . I have no more to say—except that my future life (which thank God will not endure long) must be passed in indigence and sickness—I have no energy left, nor health.

Allan did not reply. Without his foster father's help, Edgar had no way to leave West Point. He had to get himself thrown out. He began breaking as many rules as he could. He stayed in his room, missed classes and drills, earned bad marks and reprimands. Finally, the commanding officer called for a court-martial—a trial for a member of the military.

The court charged Edgar with neglect of duty and of his studies. Edgar admitted that he was guilty of all charges, and the academy dismissed him. He paid the money due for his tailoring, books, and board. With the few cents he had remaining, he prepared to return to civilian life.

Edgar made his way to New York, where he would start anew. Despite his many troubles, he felt hopeful for the future. Already his poetry had been published in Boston and in Baltimore. Another edition would appear very soon, paid for by one-dollar donations he had collected from 131 of his West Point classmates. The book might finally bring him fame and fortune. Then again, it might attract no attention at all. Few

Edgar wrote the poem "Alone" shortly after he left West Point. The poem tells of his sadness at being alone in the world. "From childhood's hour I have not been/As others were—I have not seen/As others saw—/And all I lov'd—I lov'd alone. "

people in the United States had the time or the money to spend on poetry, no matter how famous its writer. Fewer still would pay for the creations of an unknown young man. But Edgar felt certain of one thing: it was not as a cadet in a military school or as an officer in the U.S. Army that he would find the glory he deserved as a poet.

In 1831 Edgar moved into his Aunt Maria Clemm's house, above, in Baltimore, Maryland.

Chapter FOUR

BALTIMORE FAMILY

TWENTY-TWO-YEAR-OLD **EDGAR POE WANDERED** penniless through Boston and New York until the spring of 1831, when he moved to Baltimore. There he moved into the household of his aunt Maria Clemm, David Poe's sister. Maria Clemm lived in a small house on Mechanics Row with her son, Henry; her daughter, Virginia; Edgar's brother, William Henry Poe; and Edgar's grandmother, Elizabeth.

Maria Clemm was a tall, dignified, good-natured, and practical woman. Her eight-year-old daughter, Virginia, had dark eyes and long, black hair. Even as a young girl, the paleness of her skin and her large eyes gave Virginia a faraway and haunted expression.

Maria Clemm and Virginia admired Edgar. He

presented a fine appearance. He spoke well—with au-
thority and confidence. His manners were those of a
refined Southern gentleman. His eyes had a penetrat-
ing look, one that always held the attention of those
meeting or talking with him. He had a poetic senti-
ment and always spoke about the beauty of objects,
people, and words.

To provide for themselves, Maria Clemm and Virginia
usually had to rely on family and friends. Edgar felt
proud to have the new responsibility of supporting
them. He was happy that he was no longer wandering
alone in the world. He wrote letters to the editors of

*Maria Clemm provided a
much needed home for
Edgar.*

local magazines—there were dozens of them in Baltimore. He wrote to the headmasters of schools, hoping to find a position teaching literature and poetry. In reply, he received polite rejections.

His failure to find a position began to eat away at Edgar's self-confidence. Then, on August 1, 1831, his brother, William Henry Poe, died after years of sickness and alcoholism. Edgar was now the sole provider for his aunt, cousin, and the rest of the household. As the head of the household, he had to find some way to raise money. In June, he had read of a contest in the *Philadelphia Saturday Courier*. The paper would award $100 for the best short story sent to the editors. The contest inspired Edgar to try writing stories. He worked late at night on a small writing table in his house. He soon finished five tales.

The winner of the *Courier* competition was "Love's Martyr," a story by Delia Bacon. Yet the *Courier*'s editors also thought well of Edgar's stories. The next year, they published all of them. On January 14, 1832, one of the stories, "Metzengerstein," became Edgar's first-published story.

Edgar saw a new opportunity—stories are what might win him fame and fortune. Just as poetry inspired deep feelings in readers, stories could also have a strong effect. His prose could bring out a feeling of terror and mystery or the beauty of strange, unknown worlds. If chosen well, his words could stay in the memory like a haunting, unforgettable melody.

Edgar worked hard. He wrote in the evenings, when darkness fell and the streets outside his home were silent. In the spring of 1833, he finished an entire collection of stories called *Eleven Tales of the Arabesque.* In his book, the members of a club, called The Folio Club, recite the tales then discuss and critique the stories. In this way, Edgar made fun of literary critics who passed judgment on other writers.

The rejections of his works by magazines and book publishers had made Edgar bitter toward famous writers. He saw the big cities of the East—New York, Philadelphia, and Boston—as cold and self-satisfied places whose well-known writers, such as Washington Irving and James Fenimore Cooper, were merely popular men with little talent.

On June 13, 1833, the *Baltimore Saturday Visiter* announced a writing contest. The editors would award $50 for the best tale and $25 for the best poem. Edgar sent the *Visiter* six of his new stories as well as a new poem, "The Coliseum." On October 12, the *Visiter* announced the short-story winner: Edgar's "MS. Found in a Bottle." The newspaper published it one week later on its front page. The story describes a ship that encounters a terrifying storm at sea. The narrator ends the story by saying:

> [L]ittle time will be left me to ponder upon my destiny—the circles rapidly grow small—we are plunging madly within the grasp of the whirlpool—

and amid a roaring, and bellowing, and thunder-
ing of ocean and of tempest, the ship is quiver-
ing, oh God! and—going down.

With "MS. Found in a Bottle," Edgar had set out to
explore the powerful sensation of terror. He had come
to see fear of the unknown as one of the basic human
emotions. He saw many different kinds of fear—fear
of a dark room, fear of the night, fear of deranged in-
dividuals. He believed that, above all, humans felt a
terrible, deep, everlasting fear of death. He thought
such fears could provide him with the material for
fine poetry and endless story ideas. Horror of the unknown became a common theme in Edgar's works. He
began to describe nervous, obsessed, sometimes in-
sane characters who found themselves in supernatural
circumstances, coming face-to-face with death in one
gruesome form or another.

EDITOR FOR THE *MESSENGER*

Early next spring, Edgar learned that John Allan had
died on March 27, 1834. It had been many months
since Edgar had written to his foster father. A few
days after Allan's death, a lawyer read out his last will
and testament. Allan left most of his fortune and
property to his second wife, but he also gave some
money to two illegitimate children he had fathered in
Richmond. For Edgar, he left not a penny and not
even a word. Again, Edgar had been abandoned.

To try to lift his spirits, Edgar turned to John Pendleton Kennedy, an editor for the *Visiter,* for help in getting his tales published. Kennedy sent Edgar's tales to Carey, Lea, and Carey in Philadelphia and sold one of his stories to a magazine for $15. Kennedy also introduced Edgar to Thomas Wylkes White, a printer who owned the *Southern Literary Messenger,* a Richmond magazine. White asked Poe for essays, stories,

Edgar worked as an editor at the Southern Literary Messenger, a Richmond magazine, *published in the building above. The job provided him with a steady income.*

and reviews. The *Messenger*, White explained, could use a skilled writer with some knowledge of literature. White agreed to publish several of Edgar's new stories, including "Berenice" and "Morella."

"Berenice" describes a quiet man, Egaeus, who spends much of his time daydreaming. He falls in love with his cousin, Berenice, and grows fascinated by her teeth. After she becomes ill, Berenice is buried alive. Egaeus steals into her tomb at night, opens the coffin, and rips the teeth from the corpse. "Morella" is the tale of a man who can't forget his dead wife. When he blurts out her name at the christening of his daughter, the mother is reborn in the spirit of the baby.

In the summer of 1835, White hired Edgar as an editor at $10 a week. Happy to be working and earning a salary, Edgar said good-bye to Maria Clemm and Virginia and moved back to Richmond, the city where he had grown up. At the offices of the *Messenger*, in the city's downtown, he spent long hours preparing manuscripts, answering letters, and attending to business. In just a few months, the *Messenger* gained several thousand new readers. The readers liked Poe's writing and his sharp criticism of writers and their works.

MARIA CLEMM

After so many long years of struggle, Edgar was finally earning enough to buy decent clothes and to eat two or three good meals a day. Yet he still felt unhappy and lonely, and he missed his aunt and his young cousin, Virginia. He began drinking, and drank so much that White threatened to fire him. Finally, White told Edgar that he could no longer work at the *Messenger* unless he promised to stop drinking forever.

Edgar resolved to try. He knew that people depended on him. He had been sending Maria Clemm money, knowing that she was still very poor. After his grandmother, Elizabeth Poe, died in July 1835, and Maria Clemm's son, Henry, went off to sea, Aunt Maria and Virginia were living alone together.

That summer, Neilson Poe, Edgar's second cousin, wrote to invite Maria Clemm and Virginia into his household. Neilson made a good living as the owner of a newspaper in the distant town of Frederick, Maryland. Concerned for the welfare of his poor Baltimore relatives, he offered to assist Maria Clemm and see to Virginia's education and upbringing.

When Edgar heard this news, he fell into another dark, desperate depression. What would he do if Maria Clemm and Virginia left? He could not forget Virginia's large, expressive eyes and her delicate face. He could not let her go because he was desperately in love with her. He wanted to marry her. Edgar even began to fear for his life. He wrote a long, anguished letter to Maria Clemm:

> I am blinded with tears while writing this letter—
> I have no wish to live another hour. Amid sorrow,
> and the deepest anxiety your letter reached—and

you well know how little I am able to bear up under the pressure of grief. . . . But let my duty be done. I love, you know I love Virginia passion- ately devotedly. I cannot express in words the fer- vent devotion I feel towards my dear little cousin. . . . It is useless to disguise the truth that when Virginia goes with N[eilson]. P[oe]. that I shall never behold her again—that is absolutely sure. Pity me, my dear Aunty, pity me .

Maria Clemm hesitated, then agreed. She felt close to Edgar, who had taken care of her poor family as well as he could. She also knew that he saw her as a mother and as a steady, guiding hand who could help him through his bad times. She did not want to see him in despair. She decided not to move into Neilson Poe's home.

The next week, Edgar traveled to Baltimore. In Sep- tember 1835, Edgar and Virginia signed a marriage license. Virginia was only thirteen years old. Early the next month, Edgar brought the Clemm family to Richmond. In the meantime, White had written to him:

You have fine talents Edgar,—and you ought to have them respected, as well as yourself. Learn to respect yourself and you will very soon find that you are respected. Separate yourself from the bottle, and bottle companions, for ever!

In 1836 Edgar and his cousin Virginia, above, *were officially married in Baltimore.*

By the end of October 1835, Edgar had returned to the *Southern Literary Messenger.* On May 16, 1836, he married Virginia Clemm. The ceremony took place in the boardinghouse room where they lived.

People in Richmond harshly criticized Edgar for marrying the thirteen-year-old Virginia. Edgar realized that

Virginia was very young and still immature. But he was devoted to his young wife, and she felt just as strongly about him. He vowed never to abandon her as his father had abandoned his mother many years before.

While working at the Southern Literary Messenger, Edgar became famous for his scathing reviews of novels and poetry.

Chapter FIVE

NO ORDINARY CRITIC

EDGAR **A**LLAN **P**OE **WAS NO ORDINARY CRITIC, AS** the public soon learned. He sometimes praised, but more often he ridiculed. He made fun of novelists, poets, and playwrights. He criticized faults in grammar. Other writers, even those who were struggling just as he was, now had Edgar's taunting reviews to fear.

In the *Messenger*, Edgar wrote reviews of anything and everything published, from almanacs to travel diaries to scientific papers. He was especially interested in poetry. In his articles, he explained how poets should compose their verses and how their words achieved such strange and beautiful effects. Edgar's reviews drew reviews of their own. In the *Cincinnati*

Mirror, the editor wrote about the *Southern Literary Messenger:*

> Commend us to the literary notice of this magazine for genius, spice, and spirit. Those which are commendatory, are supported by the real merit of the books themselves; but woe seize on the luckless . . . who feel the savage skill with which the editor uses his tomahawk and scalping knife.

Some writers fought back with taunting letters and bad reviews of Edgar's own works. These wars of words sometimes lasted for weeks or months. Edgar enjoyed these literary duels, and his editors enjoyed the controversies he was stirring up. Rivalry and bitter feelings among writers sparked the public's interest.

Edgar was living as well as he ever had. The salary he earned at the *Southern Literary Messenger* allowed him to provide for Virginia and her mother. His health improved, and he stopped drinking. His family had enough to eat, and he could buy himself new clothes and shoes. He made a good impression on the familiar streets of Richmond, which seemed like home again.

NEW STORIES

White paid Edgar a weekly salary as well as extra money for short stories published in the *Messenger.* Edgar wrote mysteries and adventure stories and even some comic tales. "Loss of Breath" describes the uncomfortable Mr. Lackobreath, who has lost his breath on the day after his wedding. He escapes his unhappy home, only to be hanged for a murder he didn't commit. A crowd gathers at the place of execution, where Lackobreath gives the eager audience the spectacle it wants:

> My convulsions were said to be extraordinary. My spasms it would have been difficult to beat. The populace encored. Several gentlemen swooned, and a multitude of ladies were carried home in hysterics.

The writer survives his own hanging but is then buried alive. He escapes his coffin and encounters Mr. Windenough, the man who has robbed him of his breath. Angrily, he demands that Windenough return the ill-gotten breath. After he has his breath back, Lackobreath is satisfied.

A STORY AT SEA

Despite the public's attention to Edgar's stories and criticism, trouble was brewing at the *Southern Literary Messenger.* White was facing mounting debts, and the controversies that Edgar stirred up were beginning to draw criticism of the magazine itself. Edgar felt that White did not give him enough credit for the magazine's success and that he was not earning what he was worth. In January 1837, the *Messenger* announced that Edgar was leaving.

Soon afterward, Edgar moved with Virginia and Maria Clemm to New York. A bookseller, William Gowans, introduced Edgar to important writers and editors. That year also brought a financial crisis to the United States. Many magazines and newspapers went out of business, and Edgar had no luck finding a job.

Edgar's name was spreading, but no publishers had yet agreed to come out with his *Eleven Tales of the Arabesque*. Short stories didn't sell, the editors claimed. The market for books of any kind was very small. People who did read in their leisure time wanted novels, not story collections.

Edgar pressed on, trying to find a style that would attract a wide audience. He admired the stories of fantasy and horror that were fashionable in Germany at the time. He also enjoyed *Robinson Crusoe*, the famous tale of a castaway. He studied *The Rime of the Ancient Mariner*, a poem by Samuel Taylor Coleridge, and *Mutiny on the Bounty*, the true account of a violent rebellion aboard a British sailing ship. These works inspired him to create his longest work of fiction, *The Narrative of Arthur Gordon Pym*. Poe relied on the facts of a true-life expedition of an Antarctic explorer named J. N. Reynolds for this work.

Edgar's story combined adventure with science. It describes Pym, a sailor from Nantucket, Massachusetts, who experiences a series of bizarre and terrifying adventures at sea. Pym encounters pirates, mutineers, and a shipful of grinning, bedraggled corpses. Finally, he ends his voyage in the frozen seas of Antarctica.

Edgar was delighted when parts of the book were published in the *Messenger.* Soon after, in July 1838, the publisher Harper and Brothers came out with *The Narrative of Arthur Gordon Pym, of Nantucket.*

PHILADELPHIA

In the summer of 1838, Edgar moved his family to Philadelphia to seek the recognition he deserved in a new place. It was just as difficult for Edgar to find work the first year in Philadelphia as it had been in New York. But the next year, William Burton hired Edgar as the editor of *Burton's Gentlemen's Magazine.*

Burton had started *Burton's* in 1837, but the magazine was already in trouble. There was no city more competitive for publishing than Philadelphia, and the costs for paper and printing were high. Burton was losing money. He offered Edgar only $10 a week—the same amount Edgar had earned at the *Southern Literary Messenger.* Burton promised to raise Edgar's salary the next year if he stayed with the magazine. Edgar would need to spend only two hours a day at the magazine's offices. In June 1839, the two men came to an agreement. Burton hired the thirty-year-old Edgar as an assistant editor.

"Poe Walking High Bridge" is a lithograph, a type of print,
inspired by Edgar and his works. Depicting the tormented writer
trudging across a lonely bridge, the picture evokes the spooky
feelings that Edgar presented in his poetry and short stories.

Chapter **SIX**

A FIRST MYSTERY

FOR EDGAR, BURTON PROVED TO BE A BETTER
employer and a more interesting man than William
White. An experienced comic actor, Burton had played
clowns and drunks on the stages of America and England. He considered himself an English gentleman,
but he was always getting into one scandal or another.
The gossips of Philadelphia loved to spread rumors
about him, and the rumors often turned out to be true.
Burton didn't mind his scandalous fame. He believed it
might help him achieve his two ambitions: to own a
theater of his own and to publish the most popular
magazine in the United States.

In the summer of 1839, Edgar wrote nearly every review that appeared in *Burton's*. His reputation as a

ferocious critic worried his new boss, but Burton also knew he could count on Edgar for good writing.

Edgar moved his family into a comfortable home along the Schuylkill River, three miles from the center of Philadelphia. He worked long evening hours, reading, writing, and revising at his desk. He took care of his wife and his aunt, and he kept away from strong drink. He also held dinners and parties for friends and for some of his colleagues from work.

This happier and more comfortable life did not change Edgar's writing. His stories still held dark qualities of terror and the supernatural. "The Fall of the House of Usher" was printed in the September issue of *Burton's*. This gloomy tale is narrated by an anonymous young man. He arrives at the home of an old friend, Roderick Usher, whom he has not seen in many years. Usher lives in a decrepit house with his twin sister, Madeline. From his first sight of the House of Usher, a strange dread overcomes the narrator:

> I looked upon the scene before me—upon the mere house, and the simple landscape features of the domain—upon the bleak walls—upon the vacant eye-like windows—upon a few rank sedges—and upon a few white trunks of decayed trees—with an utter depression of soul. . . . There was an iciness, a sinking, a sickening of the heart—an unredeemed dreariness of thought which no goading of the imagination could torture into aught of the sublime.

This illustration of Roderick Usher and his twin sister, Madeline, appeared in a printing of "The Fall of the House of Usher." The short story is typical of Edgar's style. It is filled with suspense, gloom, and death.

The House of Usher is slowly crumbling into the swamp that surrounds it. Usher himself has the look of a corpse, with deep-set, glowing eyes that give him a terrifying expression.

Madeline dies of a strange disease. The narrator and Usher bring her coffin to a vault underneath the house. Then, one stormy night, while the narrator reads a tale out loud to calm Usher's nerves, a strange sound is heard from the vault. Madeline appears at the door of the room, after clawing her way out of the tomb where she has been buried alive. She flails about, struggling for life and breath, and kills her brother. The narrator escapes the House of Usher and sees it collapse with an eerie light and a loud noise, like a clap of thunder.

After "The Fall of the House of Usher," more of Edgar's tales appeared in *Burton's*. Edgar's name was spreading among the general public, and the publishing firm of Lea and Blanchard agreed to bring out a complete edition of his stories under the name of *Tales of the Grotesque and Arabesque*. Edgar was paid with twenty free copies of the book for this two-volume collection of twenty-five tales. Lea and Blanchard kept all the profits but also gave Poe the right to republish the stories in a book or a magazine if he wished.

Edgar was still earning very little money with the stories he worked so hard to write and perfect. Years before, he had only to provide for himself. But two other people were depending on him now. He had a simple ambition—to be a well-known writer. He was certain of his own talent, but he also felt frustrated and bitter with his failures and with an unappreciative world.

WASTED TALENTS

With Burton's permission, Edgar also contributed to other magazines. In January 1840, he challenged the readers of *Alexander's Weekly Messenger* to send him a cipher (code) that he could not solve. To make the ciphers, readers were to replace each letter of a phrase or a short passage with a different letter. Hundreds of readers took up Edgar's challenge and sent in their ciphers. Edgar solved them all, while his cipher articles drew more public attention to his talents. Edgar began to see himself not only as a writer and critic, but also as a deep thinker, a man with a talent for solving problems and puzzles of all kinds.

Edgar began to think that he was wasting his talent at *Burton's*. The steady weekly salary and freelance writing were bringing in enough money to provide for his household. But he spent most of his valuable time answering letters from readers. The magazine bored and sometimes annoyed him. Many of its articles seemed trivial and meant only to create gossip and sensation.

An answer to his problems had already occurred to the young author. He would start a magazine of his own, called *Penn*. When Burton heard about Edgar's plans, he and Edgar argued. Burton accused Edgar of planning to steal readers from *Burton's*.

Edgar had complaints, too. Burton had left all the editorial work up to Edgar, and Burton had unfairly rejected articles Edgar had written. Edgar heard that Burton was planning to sell the magazine without telling him in order to purchase a theater. Burton had once printed (and probably written himself) a review criticizing *The Narrative of Arthur Gordon Pym*. The review had appeared before Edgar joined *Burton's*— but Edgar never forgot an insult or a bad review.

After another argument, Edgar left *Burton's*. Soon afterward, Burton gave up on the magazine business. In November 1840, he sold *Burton's* to George Rex Graham, who renamed it *Graham's Magazine*.

Edgar began planning the *Penn*. He decided it
would be a national magazine. It would feature writers from all over the country—not just from the elite
centers of Boston or New York. Instead of gossip and
sensation, Edgar wanted the *Penn* to present "fearless
and honest opinion." The opinions would concern
writers and their writing. The *Penn* wouldn't bother
with politics, society news, travel stories, or other
trivial matters.

In the summer of 1840, Edgar wrote a prospectus,
which described the magazine for its future subscribers
and investors. Certain of his coming success, he put
down a list of five hundred possible subscribers suggested to him by other writers and editors. But just before the first issue of the *Penn* was to appear, in

George Rex Graham, left,
was editor of Graham's
Magazine, *for which
Edgar worked. Edgar
made plans to publish his
own magazine, the* Penn,
*while working at
Graham's.*

January 1841, another financial panic occurred. Businesses shut down, and many banks closed their doors. Paper money lost its value, and few people had spare dollars to spend on a magazine subscription. Edgar postponed the first issue of the *Penn* from January to March 1841. Then he dropped his plans altogether.

A NEW FASHION

Edgar began writing for George Rex Graham. In April 1841, *Graham's* printed "The Murders in the Rue Morgue." The tale features a skillful amateur detective, Monsieur C. Auguste Dupin. The Paris police ask Dupin to help them solve a puzzling murder that has taken place inside a locked room. Dupin carefully examines the room, the doors, the windows, the fireplace, and the courtyard outside the room. He thinks through all the possibilities and finally uncovers the murderer by using simple logic.

In "The Murders in the Rue Morgue," Edgar created an entirely new character: the amateur detective who is skilled at uncovering clues and solving crimes that the police can't solve. Edgar's story reflected important changes taking place in American society. The country was growing quickly, and more people than ever before were living in large cities. Urban living brought with it new kinds of writing. Newspaper and magazine articles described sensational crimes taking place in the cities. A new fashion in mystery stories

Edgar's "Murders in the Rue Morgue" is considered the first modern detective story. The title illustration, above, *shows an apelike monster attacking a woman, while a frightened woman watches. A murdered woman lies on the floor next to an open box of gold coins.*

was emerging, one that relied on violent plots and that posed intriguing puzzles for readers to solve.

To *Graham's* readers, "The Murders in the Rue Morgue" was more appealing than the poetry of the best Romantic writers. In just a few months, Edgar's other articles and tales helped *Graham's* increase its circulation from 3,500 to 37,000. As Edgar's name and reputation spread, *Graham's* became the most popular monthly magazine in the world.

An Unhappy Night

One night in 1842, Edgar sat down with guests in his warm and comfortable house on Coates Street. The company enjoyed a hearty meal and then gathered by the fireplace to hear Virginia sing.

Edgar felt satisfied with his life. He loved his young wife and enjoyed living with Maria Clemm. He was sure he would write more successful stories and win an even larger audience. He saw in his future higher salaries than the ordinary weekly salary Graham was paying him. He saw success for himself—soon his name would be known all over the world.

Suddenly, the music stopped. Virginia lost her voice in a fit of violent coughing. Edgar leapt forward, gathered his wife in his arms, and carried her to bed. He covered her with a coat and summoned a doctor.

The doctor examined Virginia and revealed her condition to Edgar and Maria Clemm. Virginia had fallen ill with tuberculosis, the same slow and fatal disease that had claimed Eliza Poe. As Virginia grew weaker and sicker, Edgar fell into a somber, helpless despair.

In Edgar's long poem, "The Raven," a raven visits the narrator and repeats "Nevermore!" Gustave Doré illustrated a version of the poem published in January 1845.

Chapter **SEVEN**

LITERARY
SUCCESSES

AFTER LEARNING OF VIRGINIA'S ILLNESS, EDGAR grew angry and difficult to work with. He was earning little money and still felt unappreciated despite his hard work and his good writing. Edgar knew Graham was making a profit on his magazine, but he was underpaying the members of his staff. Worse, he was doing nothing to reward the man who was doing the most to help the magazine succeed.

Edgar also grew more sensitive to criticism. He got into loud arguments with Charles Peterson, another editor at *Graham's*. One of these verbal duels ended Edgar's career with Graham. One day in April 1842, Edgar arrived to find another editor sitting in his chair and working at his desk, using his inkstand and his quill pens. Edgar turned toward the door and left the offices of *Graham's* for good.

Edgar knew there were better things in store for him. There was a chance he would soon be published in England. Just before he left *Graham's*, he had met Charles Dickens, a famous English author who was touring the United States. Edgar spoke with Dickens and gave him a copy of *Tales of the Grotesque and Arabesque*. He asked Dickens to find an English publisher for the *Tales*, and Dickens promised to try.

Edgar brought back Monsieur Dupin in another detective story, a sequel to "The Murders in the Rue Morgue." He based the new story, "The Mystery of Marie Rogêt," on the real murder of Mary Cecilia Rogers, which took place in New York. Edgar changed the name of the victim and moved the story to the streets of Paris.

A FIRM RESOLUTION

In June, Edgar left his family at home and traveled to New York to search for a job and to sell his works to other publishers. In addition to being a center for trade and manufacturing, New York had a bustling literary world. Poets and magazine editors met in bookshops to read and discuss the latest writing. Fitz-Greene Halleck, one of the city's best-known authors, wrote satires on life in New York. Evert Duyckinck edited *The Literary World* and held a salon, or gathering, for writers at his home on Clinton Place.

EDGAR ON THE SHORT STORY

F or about two hundred years, the most important and popular works of fiction have been novels. The best-known works of America's famous authors, including Mark Twain, Herman Melville, Henry James, and F. Scott Fitzgerald, are novels. But Edgar wrote only short stories, poetry, and satirical sketches. Why? Poe himself explained it in his 1842 review of *Twice-Told Tales,* a collection of stories by Nathaniel Hawthorne:

> A skillful literary artist has constructed a tale. If wise, he has not fashioned his thoughts to accommodate his incidents; but having conceived, with deliberate care, a certain unique or single effect to be wrought out, he then invents such incidents—he then combines such events as may best aid him in establishing this per-ceived effect. If his very initial sentence tends not to the outbringing of this effect, then he has failed in his first step. In the whole composition there should be no word written, of which the tendency, direct or indirect, is not to the one pre-established design. And by such means, with such care and skill, a picture is at length painted which leaves in the mind of him who contem-plates it with a kindred art, a sense of the fullest satis-faction. The idea of the tale has been presented unblemished, because undisturbed, and this is an end unattainable by the novel.

This statement reveals that, even when he wrote stories, Poe al-ways worked and thought like a poet. Edgar wanted the admi-ration of beauty to bring tears to a reader's eyes, or fear of the unknown to send a chill up a reader's spine. He wanted to bring the reader into his works and felt that he could only ac-complish this in short stories and poems. To him, novels con-tained too many characters and incidents woven into a complex plot. Edgar saw himself as a skilled painter who used the shapes and colors of words to create a portrait of the human soul.

On arriving in the city, Edgar accepted an invitation to stay with friends. In the warmth of the early summer evenings, he talked, ate, and laughed with his companions. But he also drank and lost control of himself. He walked the streets, acting strangely, talking to the buildings and sidewalks. Another spree, during which Edgar made ugly scenes in the offices of magazine editors and book publishers, lasted for days. One day, he crossed the Hudson River by ferry and began wandering through the woods of northern New Jersey. A search party found him raving and ragged and unsure of where he was.

When he returned to Philadelphia, Edgar found himself no closer to his goals. Another economic panic in the United States was ruining many banks and businesses. Nobody offered any money to invest in the magazine he still hoped to start. Desperate, Edgar finally decided to declare himself bankrupt, unable to pay his debts.

That fall, Edgar decided to try to get a different sort of job—one that would pay better than writing. He would find work as a clerk for the government. The job would be easy, he thought, and would leave him enough time to write.

In 1841 newly elected U.S. president William Henry Harrison had given his inaugural speech in a cold rainstorm. He caught pneumonia, and one month later he died. The vice president, John Tyler, succeeded him. Edgar believed the new president might

Edgar lived on Seventh Street in Philadelphia, Pennsylvania, in 1843 and 1844. The house, including the parlor, above, *has since been restored.*

appoint him as a clerk in the Philadelphia Customs House.

To get the job, Edgar wrote a letter to Frederick W. Thomas, a friend and clerk in the Treasury Department. Thomas was also a friend of Robert Tyler, the president's son. Thomas encouraged Edgar's hopes. From Washington, Thomas reported that the government might help Edgar start his own magazine if the publication would support the new administration.

In September 1842, Edgar went to Washington, D.C., to meet with Thomas and important people in the Tyler administration. Edgar hoped to meet Robert Tyler and the president himself. But again Edgar seemed to become his own worst enemy. He began to drink and to act strangely. He came down with chills and a fever. He rambled through the streets with his mud-spattered coat turned inside out. He missed his meeting with Frederick Thomas at the Congress Hall Hotel. Three weeks later, in Philadelphia, he went to the Customs House to ask about his appointment. An official curtly told him there would be no more appointments.

SCREAMS IN THE NIGHT

In January 1843, the *Pioneer* magazine of Boston published a new tale by Edgar, "The Tell-Tale Heart." The story began:

> True!—nervous—very, very dreadfully nervous I had been and am; but why will you say that I am mad? The disease had sharpened my senses—not destroyed—not dulled them. Above all was the sense of hearing acute. I heard all things in the heaven and in the earth. I heard many things in hell. How, then, am I mad? Hearken! and observe how healthily—how calmly I can tell you the whole story.

The narrator, in a state of frenzy, murders an old man in his bed and cuts apart the corpse. He hides the body parts beneath the floorboards of the room so nobody will be able to detect the evil deed. The secret is safe, even as police detectives arrive to investigate a report by neighbors who have heard a scream coming from the house in the middle of the night.

The police take their chairs and begin asking questions. Suddenly, a low, dull, quick sound begins to rise from beneath the floor. The narrator gasps for breath,

Edgar's short story of horror, "The Tell-Tale Heart," tells how a crafty murderer kills a man and hears the dead man's heart beating underneath the floorboards.

but the police seem to hear nothing. Finally, the murderer can stand it no more:

> Villains! . . . I admit the deed!—tear up the planks! here, here!—it is the beating of his hideous heart!

The ghoulish "Tell-Tale Heart" thrilled and terrified Edgar's readers. Such a story made the public very curious about its author. Edgar must be quite strange, they thought, perhaps even evil. What must he be hiding behind his carefully chosen words? What strange sounds must be echoing in his head?

THE GOTHIC ROMANCE

I n Edgar Allan Poe's lifetime, a new style of writing known as Gothic Romance grew popular with readers in Europe and the United States. Gothic writing began to evolve in the novels and poetry of late eighteenth-century England. A group of English writers, including Horace Walpole, who wrote *The Castle of Otranto,* and Ann Ward Radcliffe, author of *The Mysteries of Udolpho,* set their tales in haunted castles or medieval abbeys. They created dark, ghostly, terrifying tales that thrilled and frightened their readers.

Gothic writing reached the United States in the early nineteenth century. The leading American Gothic writer was Charles Brockden Brown, who wrote *Edgar Huntly,* a novel that describes a hero who falls into a deep, dark pit. This tale inspired Poe to write "The Pit and the Pendulum," one of his best-known short stories. Poe used many Gothic devices in his stories, but his remarkable ability to describe characters and establish a mood set him well above the Gothic writers whom the modern reading public has since forgotten.

Readers worldwide in the twenty-first century still know the most famous Gothic tales, even if they have never actually read them. These are *Frankenstein,* by the young English writer Mary Wollstonecraft Shelley, and *Dracula,* by the Irishman Bram Stoker. *Frankenstein* and *Dracula* were among the first Gothic novels to be turned into Hollywood movies. They were also the first of a very long line of horror films, a genre that remains alive in works such as *Halloween, Night of the Living Dead,* and *Scream.*

THE GOLD BUG

Edgar renamed his hoped-for magazine *The Stylus.* Thomas C. Clarke, a wealthy Philadelphia publisher, agreed to help him publish it. In the meantime, Edgar finished "The Gold Bug," a story describing a mysterious treasure hunt on a South Carolina island. He wanted to print the story in the first issue of *The Stylus,* but he didn't have the funds. When *The Dollar Newspaper* announced a short-story contest that would award $100 for first place, Edgar sent in the story. "The Gold Bug" won the prize and appeared in *The Dollar Newspaper* on June 28, 1843.

"The Gold Bug," which covered the entire front page of the newspaper, made Edgar famous throughout the United States. In response to this first "best-seller," Graham agreed to bring out a new edition of Poe's works, named *The Prose Romances of Edgar A. Poe.* It was to be the first in a series of books. The first edition appeared later in 1843 and included "The Murders in the Rue Morgue" and "The Man That Was Used Up."

Although Edgar and Graham had made plans to print more editions, there turned out to be only a single edition of *The Prose Romances of Edgar A. Poe.* Story collections were still not selling well. Readers continued to prefer stories that appeared only in magazines. Such stories were brief entertainment, to be enjoyed while sitting for an hour by the evening fire.

THE PIT AND "THE RAVEN"

In the fall of 1843, Edgar published another gruesome story, "The Pit and the Pendulum." The nightmarish tale describes a prisoner trapped in a pitch-black dungeon. He stumbles along the walls, desperately trying to understand the size and shape of his cell. He falls unconscious, then wakes to find himself strapped to a slab of stone, with a sharp blade swinging above his chest, slowly descending. As the blade slices at his clothing and ravenous rats swarm around him, he makes a frenzied last effort to save himself.

Even though his stories were catching on with the public, Edgar still considered himself a poet. For him, composing good poetry was the greatest challenge for any writer. In late 1843, he began to work on a new poem.

Edgar set down the poem in seventeen stanzas. He carefully arranged its words and syntax, finding a hypnotic rhythm that brought out his feelings of sadness, fear, and regret. For weeks, he struggled to describe his vision of a somber room and a winged messenger that sings a single, mysterious word. Edgar wanted this work to evoke bitter memories of a long-lost love. He read "The Raven" to friends and editors, then brought the poem down to the offices of *Graham's*. He recited it while Graham and his entire staff listened.

> Once upon a midnight dreary, while I pondered,
> weak and weary,

Over many a quaint and curious volume of
  forgotten lore—
While I nodded, nearly napping, suddenly there
  came a tapping,
As of some one gently rapping, rapping at my
  chamber door.
'Tis some visitor,' I muttered, 'tapping at my
  chamber door—
    Only this and nothing more.'

The narrator of the poem spends many hours here,
trying to forget a woman named Lenore, whom
he has lost forever. To discover where the strange tapping comes from, he flings open a shutter, and a black
raven flies into the room. The bird perches on a
marble statue of Pallas, a figure from ancient
Greek mythology. The bird can speak only one word:
"Nevermore!"

Then, upon the velvet sinking, I betook myself to
  linking
Fancy unto fancy, thinking what this ominous
  bird of yore—
What this grim, ungainly, ghastly, gaunt, and
  ominous bird of yore
    Meant in croaking "Nevermore."

The air in the room grows thick. The narrator screams
angrily at the bird and demands to know what it means

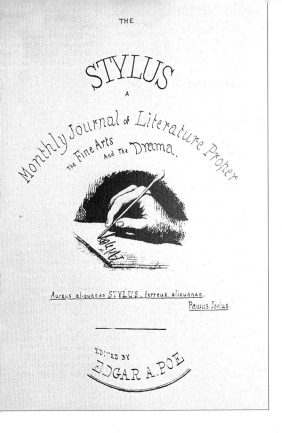

THE

STYLUS
A
Monthly Journal of Literature Proper
The Fine Arts And The Drama.

Aureus aliquando STYLUS, ferreus aliquando.
Paulus Jovius.

EDITED BY
EDGAR A. POE

Edgar's magazine, The Stylus, *barely got off the ground and never made a profit.*

by that single word. Why has the bird invaded his room and what does it mean by its croaking?

And the Raven, never flitting, still is sitting, still
  is sitting.
On the pallid bust of Pallas just above my
  chamber door;
And his eyes have all the seeming of a demon's
  that is dreaming,
And the lamplight o'er him streaming throws his
  shadow on the floor;
And my soul from out that shadow that lies
  floating on the floor
      Shall be lifted—nevermore!

After Edgar finished the recital, the men at the offices of *Graham's* muttered their disappointment. They pitied Edgar for writing such a ridiculous poem. The magazine would not publish it, but the editors "passed the hat" for the author. They collected $15 and gave the money to Edgar. Humiliated, Edgar accepted the money and turned himself out of the office, still holding the rejected "Raven" in his hands.

Edgar decided to leave Philadelphia for good. His own magazine, *The Stylus,* was coming to nothing, even with the promised support of Thomas Clarke. He returned to New York, where he found a boarding-house on Greenwich Street. He brought Virginia to the house, where the two received a warm welcome from the owner and his wife. (Maria Clemm would come as soon as they were settled.) That night, Mr. and Mrs. Poe ate well, better than they had in many weeks.

Edgar's goal was to make his fortune in New York, a city that was bigger, richer, and perhaps more understanding of his talent than Philadelphia. He planned to sell his works to the *Knickerbocker* and other New York magazines. In this busy city, where everyone seemed to have a business or was starting one, he would raise enough money to begin his own magazine.

Edgar may have drawn this self-portrait around 1845, at the age of thirty-six.

Chapter **EIGHT**

HORROR

AT FIRST NEW YORK PRESENTED NO BETTER
opportunity than Philadelphia. Edgar fell ill and spent
many days lying in bed. Virginia's illness often prevented her from leaving the house. Maria Clemm
walked through the large city, calling on editors and
publishers, trying to help her son-in-law. In the fall of
1844, she called on Nathaniel Willis, the editor of the
New York Evening Mirror, at his office. Willis agreed
to hire Edgar as a contributor at a salary of $15 a
week.

Edgar wrote hundreds of short "fillers" for the *Mirror.* Most of these articles just gossiped about famous
writers or actors. Edgar didn't mind gossiping about
famous people, but he quickly grew bored with

writing about them. Most of the fillers did not even name the author. His work for the *Mirror* did nothing for Edgar's reputation among the public or the critics.

But on January 29, 1845, the *Mirror* printed the poem that would make thirty-six-year-old Edgar one of the most famous writers in the country. *The Raven* appeared in a single long column on the *Mirror's* back page. Soon afterward, other newspapers in New York, Boston, Philadelphia, and every other large city reprinted the poem.

MOVING TO THE BROADWAY JOURNAL

The success of *The Raven* led Edgar to believe that his writings would make a success of any magazine he joined. His confidence prompted him to make an agreement with the owners of the *Broadway Journal*. They would pay him one-third of the magazine's profits instead of a weekly salary. In exchange, he would provide at least one page of material for each new issue.

Edgar moved from the offices of the *Mirror* to the *Journal*. To supply his weekly quota of material, he reprinted many of his tales and poems. He wrote reviews of books and plays and commented on the literary scene. He worked hard, often staying at his desk well into the evening. He hoped to turn the fame he had won with *The Raven* and "The Gold Bug" into fortune, or at least a good, comfortable living.

Despite all of his hard work, Edgar found himself

Edgar was frustrated with the fame achieved by writers Henry Wadsworth Longfellow, above left, *and Ralph Waldo Emerson,* above right.

earning one-third of almost nothing, as the *Journal* barely made a profit. Through the summer of 1845, his frustration grew worse. Edgar began to realize that it was almost impossible for a writer in the United States to support himself by writing. The public still saw books as a luxury. There were few bookstores, even in large cities, and even fewer that sold collections of poems or short stories. And newspapers and magazines paid very little money to their contributors.

Edgar began drinking again and going on aimless sprees, angering his friends and colleagues. He could not stand to see other writers, such as Henry Longfellow, Ralph Waldo Emerson, and James Russell Lowell, earn more praise and money than he did. He watched the

TRANSCENDENTALISM

When Edgar Allan Poe was alive, the best-known writers of the United States lived in New England—particularly in Boston and Cambridge, Massachusetts. Many, including Ralph Waldo Emerson and Henry David Thoreau, belonged to a movement called Transcendentalism. Transcendentalists opposed the strict teachings of Calvinism, a Protestant church that taught that people were naturally sinful and must be saved. Transcendentalists believed that human beings could appreciate beauty and discover truth outside of the Protestant Church. All they needed was a pure spirit that "transcended" ordinary, day-to-day worries and habits.

Many of the Transcendentalists were ministers. Their church, called the Unitarian Church, held that humans were self-reliant and could shape their own destiny without following religious doctrines.

The Transcendentalists published journals, held meetings, founded self-sufficient communities in the countryside, and formed clubs. Poe, however, did not belong to any Transcendentalist clubs. Poe saw the New Englanders as snobby, wealthy, and self-satisfied members of a northern community that would never welcome him, a southerner of humble origins. He did not sympathize with their social concerns, such as temperance (abstaining from liquor), women's rights, and the abolition of slavery. He didn't care for churches, whether Unitarian or Calvinist. And he didn't address social movements or new philosophies in any of his fiction. His goal was to trigger strong sensations of fear or the appreciation of beauty in his readers.

fame he had earned with "The Raven" slip away and grew enraged at his own poverty. He saw others slighting him at every turn and imagined his rivals plotting his destruction. He felt alone again, as he had felt in Richmond after storming away from John Allan's home. Once again, the world grew dark and threatening.

A RETURN TO BOSTON

Edgar knew there was more than one way to earn a living by writing. Many people in cities around the United States enjoyed attending evening lectures. Writers, editors, politicians, philosophers, and European visitors appeared in public halls, delivering speeches on virtually any topic. They earned a percentage of the money earned by the ticket sales.

That fall, Edgar arranged to give a lecture in Boston. Even though he had been born there, Edgar saw Boston as enemy territory. It was the home of the nation's best-known writers and critics, most of whom he saw as snobs. Boston was hostile to Edgar's childhood home, Virginia and the South, and its people strongly disapproved of slavery, which was still legal in Virginia.

Edgar announced that he would write a new poem for the appearance, one that would be as good as "The Raven." But try as he might, he found no inspiration to write the new poem. On the evening of October 16, he arrived in Boston. That night, he gave a long and dreary performance. Instead of delivering a new poem, he recited *Al Aaraaf,* a work he had written almost twenty years earlier. Edgar recited the poem's 260 lines in front of an impatient audience, almost as if he wanted to anger them and make a fool of himself. Most of the audience walked out of the hall before he finally recited "The Raven."

The city's reviewers ridiculed his Boston appearance. Edgar knew they would. He did not mind letting his readers know he disliked New Englanders, so he answered the criticism with a sarcastic notice in the *Broadway Journal:*

> We like Boston. We were born there—and perhaps it is just as well not to mention that we are heartily ashamed of the fact. The Bostonians are very well in their way. Their hotels are bad. Their pumpkin pies are delicious. Their poetry is not so good. . . . But with all these good qualities the Bostonians have no soul. . . . The Bostonians are well-bred—as very dull persons generally are. . . .

A MAGAZINE OF HIS OWN

By the fall of 1845, Charles Briggs, co-owner of the *Broadway Journal,* was growing tired of Edgar's drinking, as well as his writing and his reviews. Since Briggs wanted to get out of the magazine business anyway, he allowed Edgar and John Bisco, another *Journal* editor, to buy his share of the magazine. Bisco and Edgar then became partners.

Edgar saw this as his opportunity to finally run a magazine of his own. But the *Journal* was in deep financial trouble. There were printers and typesetters to pay, and there was very little money in the magazine's bank account. When Bisco decided to give up his share for a payment of $50, Edgar suddenly became the sole owner of the *Broadway Journal*. He wrote to old friends and even to some old enemies, begging for money to help him keep the magazine going. Horace Greeley, editor of the *New York Tribune*, agreed to loan him $50. On October 26, 1845, Edgar wrote to his Philadelphia acquaintance Rufus Griswold, who had not been friendly to him:

> Will you aid me at a pinch—at one of the greatest pinches conceivable? If you will, I will be indebted to you, for life. After a prodigious deal of maneuvering, I have succeeded in getting the "Broadway Journal" entirely within my own control. It will be a fortune to me if I can hold it— and I can do it easily with a very trifling aid from my friends. May I count you as one? Lend me $50 and you shall never have cause to regret it.

In spite of these efforts, Edgar could not find the money to pay contributors. And he found himself overwhelmed with all the tasks of getting out the *Journal*. Because he was too busy to write new material, he simply reprinted old poems and tales. By the

Maria Clemm, Virginia, and Edgar moved to a cottage outside New York City, where Edgar wrote a column for Godey's magazine.

end of the year, he realized the magazine was failing. He signed over half-ownership of the *Journal* to Thomas Lane, a friend from Philadelphia. On January 3, Lane decided to close down the *Journal* for good.

A TALE OF REVENGE

In May 1846, Edgar again escaped New York. He moved Maria Clemm and the frail Virginia away from the city's noise and dirt and into the fresh air and quiet of the countryside. The family rented a small farm in Fordham, fourteen miles north of New York City. In the same month, Edgar began writing a new column for *Godey's* magazine in Philadelphia. He passed along gossip about New York literary figures.

Edgar also made some enemies with his remarks and his gossip. Among them was Thomas Dunn English, a poet and doctor from Philadelphia who carried on a vicious literary duel with Edgar. English spread rumors of Edgar's poor character and accused him of forgery. When Edgar proved that the charge was false, English repeated it, daring Edgar to sue him. Edgar sued him in July 1846. Eventually, Edgar won the lawsuit and collected a small sum for damage done to his reputation.

In the fall of 1846, he finished a new story, "The Cask of Amontillado," about the deep desire for revenge. At the beginning of the story, the character of Montresor explains his dark purpose:

> The thousand injuries of Fortunato I had borne as I best could, but when he ventured upon insult I vowed revenge. You, who so well know the nature of my soul, will not suppose, however, that I gave utterance to a threat. At length I would be avenged—this was a point definitely settled. . . . I must not only punish but punish with impunity.

Montresor lures his enemy to a cellar with the promise of a taste of the finest Amontillado wine. Fortunato agrees; it is carnival time, he has been drinking, and he is dressed in a clown costume. In the cellar, Montresor chains Fortunato to a wall. He begins laying a brick wall that will seal Fortunato's tomb and assure him a death by hunger, thirst, and fear.

> My heart grew sick—it was the dampness of the catacombs that made it so. I hastened to make an end of my labour. I forced the last stone into its position; I plastered it up. Against the new masonry I re-erected the old rampart of bones. For the half of a century no mortal has disturbed them.

A DEATH AT HOME

"The Cask of Amontillado" appeared in November 1846, in the pages of *Godey's* magazine. But soon Edgar would have another horrible reason to feel sad and bitter. Winter was coming, and the cold, damp weather was worsening his young wife's condition. She was dying, and Edgar could not even afford to give her comfortable bedding. Virginia slept on a bed of straw, covered with the old military coat Edgar had worn at West Point.

Friends collected some money and brought it to the house so that Edgar could give his wife linen sheets and a more comfortable bed. On December 15, 1846, a notice was published in the *New York Express,* asking for help for the Poes. Some admirers of Edgar passed money to him anonymously. But there was no amount of money that could cure Virginia's illness, and there was nothing any doctor could do. Edgar and Maria Clemm watched helplessly as Virginia slipped away on January 30, 1847. Edgar described the death of his wife in a letter to a friend:

> Her life was despaired of. I took leave of her forever and underwent all the agonies of her death. She recovered partially, and I again hoped. At the end of a year, the [blood] vessel broke again. I went through precisely the same scene. . . . Each time I felt the agonies of her death—and at each accession of the disorder I loved her more dearly and clung to her life with more desperate pertinacity. But I am constitutionally sensitive— nervous in a very unusual degree. I became insane, with long intervals of horrible sanity. During these fits of absolute unconsciousness, I drank—God only knows how often or how much.

On January 31, Edgar placed his wife's open coffin on his writing table for viewing, as was customary at that time. Neighbors arrived to pay their last respects, and a small procession began outside. Edgar buried his wife in the graveyard of the Fordham Dutch Reformed Church.

Virginia's death turned Edgar into a silent, mourning shadow. He wandered through the house like a ghost. In the worst moments of grief, he drowned his sorrows with drink.

Edgar had this daguerreotype (a type of photograph) taken in 1848 for Sarah Helen Whitman, a woman he courted after Virginia's death.

Chapter **NINE**

REJECTION

AFTER VIRGINIA'S DEATH, EDGAR SPENT MOST OF his time at the Fordham cottage he shared with Maria Clemm. Most of the time, he felt too ill or depressed to leave the house. His troubled mind prevented him from working and often from sleeping. To relieve his depression, he took nighttime walks to Virginia's nearby tomb. He would sit there for hours on end, not moving or speaking.

To help Edgar, Nathaniel Willis printed Edgar's poems and reviews in the *Mirror*. Maria Clemm, meanwhile, walked around the city, calling on friends and editors. She collected money for the household by begging or by selling letters Poe had received from other writers.

Eureka!

Edgar slowly recovered from the loss of Virginia. In the summer of 1847, he began planning a triumphant return to New York City. He worked on an essay, which he planned to read at a lecture in New York to raise money for *The Stylus*.

Within months, Edgar was finishing his essay, which he called "Eureka." In this work, Edgar tried to explain the secrets of nature—of the galaxies, the stars, the Sun, the Moon, and the planets. Edgar intended "Eureka" to be a work of science and philosophy, where he would reveal the divine plan that had created the universe. But instead of equations or measurements, Edgar used his own intuition and his poetic inspiration.

In its poetic way, "Eureka" predicted two important theories of modern physics: the big bang, in which all the matter in the universe is thought to have originated in a powerful explosion billions of years ago; and the big crunch, in which the universe will, some time far in the future, shrink back to a single point.

But Edgar's lecture and reading of "Eureka" was a big failure. On the night he was to give the reading, a fierce winter storm hit New York. Only sixty people fought their way through the ice and snow to come to the lecture, and Edgar hardly made a cent. Few people could understand "Eureka." It was a work that seemed to fly over their heads. They felt Edgar was mocking their intelligence with his strange ideas.

AN ADMIRING RAVEN

Edgar's tales and poems still drew a large audience in the United States and in Europe. Many readers wrote to him to express their admiration. Among them were many female admirers, fascinated by Edgar's gallant appearance, his mysterious writings, and his tragic personal life. Poe returned their attention. He felt lonely after Virginia's death, and he enjoyed the company of women.

In February 1848, Edgar received a poem from one of these admirers. The sender had titled her work "To Edgar A. Poe." The writer imitated Edgar's own style in "The Raven," even borrowing some of its phrases and rhymes. Edgar soon discovered the poet's identity and answered her compliments with a poem of his own, calling it "To Helen."

Edgar remembered first seeing Sarah Helen Whitman in 1845, while he was visiting Providence, Rhode Island. Sarah wrote and published poetry, and many critics admired her work. When he learned that Sarah had written the admiring poem, Edgar grew anxious to see her again.

In September 1848, he left New York for Providence. He arrived at Sarah's front door, spoke with her, quickly fell in love, and proposed marriage. Although her mother and the rest of her family disapproved of Edgar, Sarah sent him away with a promise to consider his proposal.

After Edgar left Providence, many of Sarah's friends

began talking behind his back. They warned her that Edgar was an untrustworthy drunkard. He was poor, he had no future prospects, and he had many enemies. The true reason for his proposal was hardly love. Instead, they said, it was the Whitman family money, which Sarah would soon inherit.

In the first week of November, Edgar returned to Providence, this time ill and feverish. After seeing him this way, Sarah's mother and sister firmly set themselves against the marriage. But Sarah agreed to marry Edgar as long as he promised to stop drinking. Edgar made the promise, but his words did not satisfy Sarah's angry mother. She threatened to cut Sarah out of her will if the marriage took place.

Edgar hoped to marry poet and admirer Sarah Helen Whitman.

Edgar still pressed Sarah to marry him. He returned to Providence on December 20, 1848. Once again, he asked Sarah Whitman to marry him. But then, while Sarah was sitting in a public library, a clerk passed her an anonymous letter. The letter accused Edgar of breaking his promise not to drink. Although she still loved and admired Edgar, Sarah grew uneasy. She decided not to go through with the marriage. Edgar left Providence, disappointed.

TALE OF A JESTER

In the meantime, Edgar had been working on another tale of bitter revenge, "Hop-Frog." The story takes place in the castle of a cruel king who loves jokes made at the expense of others. One evening, the king's jester, a dwarf named Hop-Frog, is forced to drink wine, though the jester can't stand wine. When a young girl, Trippetta, begs the king to stop the joke, the king throws his goblet of wine in her face.

Later, the king calls on Hop-Frog to prepare for a masquerade (costume party). The jester agrees and plans his revenge. He asks the king and seven of the king's ministers to dress as orangutans and tells them that they will play a joke on the other guests. Hop-Frog chains the eight men together and covers their costumes with tar and flax. As the masquerade reaches its noisiest point, the orangutans enter the hall, causing a great commotion. They gather in the center of the room, gesturing wildly, screaming, scattering the guests to and fro. The king and his ministers enjoy the great joke.

Suddenly, Hop-Frog pulls the eight men up by the chains that bind them. They hang suspended from the ceiling, while he sets them on fire with a burning torch. The king and his ministers are burned alive in their costumes, dying hideous, screaming deaths. Silently, the guests watch the terrible spectacle taking place over their heads.

> The eight corpses swung in their chains, a fetid, blackened, hideous, and indistinguishable mass. The cripple hurled his torch at them, clambered leisurely to the ceiling, and disappeared through the sky-light.

> It is supposed that Trippetta, stationed on the roof of the saloon, had been the accomplice of her friend in his fiery revenge, and that, together, they effected their escape to their own country; for neither was seen again.

AN IDEA FROM THE WEST

In December 1848, a Boston magazine called *The Flag of Our Union* published "Hop-Frog." That same month, Edgar received a letter from E. H. N. Patterson, who lived in the small town of Oquawka, Illinois. Patterson wanted to start a literary journal, and he wanted Edgar to be his editor. Edgar wrote back, revealing the many ideas he had collected over the years for *The Stylus*. Claiming he could gather twenty thousand subscribers, Edgar asked Patterson for a loan of $50 so that he could make a lecture tour through the South. He would give speeches to raise interest in the new journal.

Poe thought he might work with Patterson but believed that Oquawka was no place to publish a literary magazine. He asked Patterson to move his office to St. Louis, Missouri. Edgar wanted the new magazine to target southern and western readers and to feature poets, essayists, and storytellers who were not from New York or Boston, traditional centers of American writing.

He still felt alone in the northeast, an outcast from the clique of writers and editors that dominated the country's literature. He also felt himself growing alienated from New York and from all of its money-hungry people. Edgar still saw himself as a Southerner. He was a stranger in these cold northern cities, a man who put his honor, good manners, and style above the desire for money.

GOING BACK TO RICHMOND

Virginia's death and Sarah Whitman's rejection still agonized Edgar. He felt like a failure in his personal and professional life. He began to lose his fear of death and to think of it as a release from his bitterness and suffering.

In 1849 Mrs. Elmira Shelton, left, and Edgar renewed their relationship.

In early July 1849, on his way to Richmond, he stopped in Philadelphia and went on another drinking spree. He grew violently ill and started hearing voices. He hallucinated and was certain that a group of men was trying to kill him. The police arrested Edgar and threw him in jail for drunkenness. After his release, he returned to the Philadelphia train depot to claim his suitcase, which had been lost for ten days. To his dismay, the lectures he planned to deliver on his tour through the South had been stolen.

Finally, Edgar reached Richmond, where he moved into a hotel. He took a solemn vow to stop drinking for good. He also called on Sarah Elmira Royster, the girl he had written to from the University of Virginia. She was a wealthy widow named Mrs. Shelton, but she had not forgotten the love she had felt for Poe twenty years earlier. She and Edgar renewed their friendship. The two began planning a possible marriage.

Edgar delivered successful lectures in Richmond and Norfolk, Virginia. On September 27, 1849, he boarded a steamer at the Richmond harbor. He planned to stop in Baltimore, then continue on to New York. He would rescue Maria Clemm from the sad, solitary house in Fordham. He would pack his things, close up the house and return to Richmond. After all the sadness and misfortune, he would return to old friends, a loyal audience for his works and his lectures, and an almost-forgotten love.

Edgar traveled to Baltimore, above, on his way to New York City and stopped to rest in Philadelphia. He then mistakenly ended up in Baltimore again.

Chapter **TEN**

REYNOLDS

ON **SEPTEMBER 28, 1849,** THE STEAMER CARRY-
ing Edgar Allan Poe from Richmond pulled up to a
wharf in Baltimore's harbor and let off its passengers.
It was growing rainy and cold in the city, and Edgar
already felt very ill. In a hurry to complete his voyage
to New York, he caught a train for Philadelphia.
There, he was welcomed at the home of James P.
Moss, a relative of Thomas Lane and an old friend of
Edgar's. Edgar was feverish, and Moss allowed him to
rest and recover from the difficult journey. When he
felt well enough to travel again, Edgar returned to the
Philadelphia train station. But instead of catching the
train to New York, he mistakenly boarded a train
headed in the opposite direction—back to Baltimore.

Wednesday, October 3, was election day in Baltimore. Candidates for the U.S. Congress, the Maryland legislature, and Baltimore's city offices were collecting votes. On that day, just outside one of the polls, Poe ran into Joseph Walker, who worked for the *Baltimore Sun*. Walker questioned the trembling and half-conscious Edgar. Edgar was sick and delirious, but he managed to pronounce the name of Joseph Snodgrass, the editor of the *Baltimore Saturday Visiter*. Walker quickly scribbled a note:

> Dear Sir,
> There is a gentleman, rather the worse for wear, at Ryan's 4th ward polls, who goes under the cognomen [name] of Edgar A. Poe, and who appears in great distress, and he says he is acquainted with you, and I assure you he is in need of immediate assistance.
> Yours, in haste,
> Jos. W. Walker

Snodgrass hurried over to where Edgar was. He found Edgar inside a tavern, helplessly confused and sick in an armchair. His hair was unkempt and his clothes were dirty and ragged.

Henry Herring, the husband of Maria Clemm's sister, arrived soon after Snodgrass. The two men took Edgar to the Washington Medical College, where he was checked into a ward for drunkards. Dr. John J. Moran, who knew and admired Edgar's works, examined the patient. Nurses and orderlies stopped their work to glance into the room. They also knew Edgar from his mysterious stories, his poetry, and his biting reviews. As they and Dr. Moran watched, Edgar talked to the walls and windows. His arms and legs shook uncontrollably while his vacant eyes sank back into his ghostly face.

For three days, Edgar drifted in and out of consciousness. Dr. Moran could do nothing for his patient but keep him as comfortable as possible. While Edgar stayed in the hospital, no word was passed to Maria Clemm or to anyone in Richmond. As far as his friends and family knew, he had simply disappeared.

Early in the morning on Sunday, October 7, Edgar started shouting out the name "Reynolds" while the bewildered nurses and Dr. Moran tried to quiet him. Was this the name of Jeremiah Reynolds, who had once made a voyage of discovery to the South Pole? Long ago, Reynolds had inspired Edgar to write *The Narrative of Arthur Gordon Pym*, in which a mariner drifts helplessly southward, toward the white mists and icy Antarctic waters that meant death.

Finally, about five o'clock that morning, the forty-year-old Edgar stopped his strange and terrifying chant. He suddenly came to, whispered "Lord help my poor soul!" and died.

Edgar's tomb is in Baltimore.

EPILOGUE

On the afternoon of October 9, 1849, Edgar Allan Poe was buried in the Presbyterian Cemetery of Baltimore. The Reverend W. T. D. Clemm gave a funeral service to a small group. Twenty-six years later, Edgar's body was moved to a new grave in the same cemetery, where he lies beside the bodies of Virginia and Maria Clemm.

A few short notices of Edgar's death ran in the newspapers of Baltimore, New York, and Philadelphia. In Richmond, newspaper and journal editors wrote long and admiring eulogies. To them, Edgar was a son of the South, a man of talent and deep sentiments. He represented an alternative to the cold and logical writers of the North. The cities of Philadelphia, Baltimore, and Richmond raised memorials to Edgar, proudly claiming him as one of their own. Devoted readers made pilgrimages to Edgar's grave in the Presbyterian Cemetery.

In the years after his death, Edgar gained a wide audience in foreign countries. The French poet Charles-Pierre Baudelaire translated Edgar's stories and poems. Baudelaire's work made Edgar the most popular American author in France. British writers also admired Edgar. The French detective C. Auguste Dupin, who appeared in "The Murders in the Rue Morgue" and two other Edgar Allan Poe stories, had a

These modern book covers of Edgar's works show the telltale elements of mystery, gore, and terror in Edgar's writing.

very strong influence on Sir Arthur Conan Doyle, a young British writer. Doyle borrowed many of Dupin's traits to create his own fictional sleuth, Sherlock Holmes of London. By the end of the nineteenth century, readers in Spain, Germany, Russia, Italy, Portugal, and other nations were reading Edgar's stories and poetry.

Edgar grew even more popular in the twentieth century. His horror stories found a worldwide audience, while the public forgot about writers who had been much more successful than Edgar in his day. School-teachers assigned Edgar's stories and poems to their students. Hollywood directors created lurid films from "The Fall of the House of Usher" and "The Pit and the Pendulum." Edgar's name became synonymous with the popular horror genre.

Edgar's strange, supernatural tales provide an escape from the real world. Many modern readers sympathize with Edgar's struggles, his search for fame, his love of beauty, and his feelings of isolation from the rest of society. The terrifying phantoms, gloomy castles, and grim dungeons that Edgar created are as fascinating as his exploration of the human soul, with all its strange fears and desires. Something in Edgar's writing speaks directly to the reader, as if the long-dead writer himself were sitting close by, whispering feverishly from within his quiet marble tomb.

SOURCES

10-11 Arthur Hobson Quinn, *Edgar Allan Poe: A Critical Biography* (Baltimore: The Johns Hopkins Press, 1998), 44.

22-23 John Ward Ostrom, ed., *The Letters of Edgar Allan Poe* (New York: Gordian Press, Inc., 1966), 7–8.

32 Quinn, 172.

38-39 Edgar Allan Poe, *Selected Writings of Edgar Allan Poe,* edited with an introduction by David Galloway (New York: Penguin Books, 1977), 109.

42-43 Quinn, 219.

43 Ibid., 229.

48 Kenneth Silverman, *Edgar A. Poe: Mournful and Never-ending Remembrance* (New York: HarperCollins, 1991), 122.

49 Edgar Allan Poe, *The Other Poe: Comedies and Satires,* edited with an introduction by David Galloway (New York: Penguin Books, 1983), 38.

54 Poe, *Selected Writings,* 138.

68 Ibid., 277.

69 Ibid., 282.

72 Ibid., 77–80.

82 Quinn, 487.

83 Ostrom, 298.

85 Poe, *Selected Writings,* 360.

86 Ibid., 366.

87 Wolf Mankowitz, *The Extraordinary Mr. Poe* (New York: Summit Books, 1978), 141.

94 Poe, *Selected Writings,* 376.

100 Quinn, 638.

BIBLIOGRAPHY

Allen, Hervey Israfel. *The Life and Times of Edgar Allan Poe*. New York: Farrar and Rinehart, Inc., 1934.

Anderson, Madelyn Klein. *Edgar Allan Poe: A Mystery*. New York: Franklin Watts, 1993.

Bittner, William. *Poe: A Biography*. Boston: Little, Brown, 1962.

Buranelli, Vincent. *Edgar Allan Poe*. Twayne's United States Authors series. Boston: Twayne Publishers, 1977.

The Cambridge History of American Literature. New York: The Macmillan Company, 1943.

Canby, Henry Seidel. *Classic Americans: A Study of Eminent American Writers from Irving to Whitman*. New York: Russell and Russell, 1959.

Jacobs, William Jay. *Edgar Allan Poe: Genius in Torment*. New York: McGraw Hill, 1975.

Knapp, Bettina. *Edgar Allan Poe*. New York: F. Unger, 1984.

LeVert, Suzanne. *Edgar Allan Poe*. Philadelphia: Chelsea House, 1992.

Loewen, Nancy. *Poe*. Mankato, MN: Creative Education, 1993.

Mankowitz, Wolf. *The Extraordinary Mr. Poe*. New York: Summit Books, 1978.

Ostrom, John Ward, ed. *The Letters of Edgar Allan Poe*. New York: Gordian Press, Inc., 1966.

Poe, Edgar Allan. *The Other Poe: Comedies and Satires*. Edited with an introduction by David Galloway. New York: Penguin Books, 1983.

Poe, Edgar Allan. *Selected Writings of Edgar Allan Poe*. Edited with an introduction by David Galloway. New York: Penguin Books, 1977.

Quinn, Arthur Hobson. *Edgar Allan Poe: A Critical Biography*. Baltimore: The Johns Hopkins Press, 1998.

Shorto, Russell. *Edgar Allan Poe: Creator of Dreams*. New York: Kipling Press, 1988.

Silverman, Kenneth. *Edgar A. Poe: Mournful and Never-ending Remembrance*. New York: HarperCollins, 1991.

Stem, Philip Van Doren. *Edgar Allan Poe, Visitor from the Night of Time*. New York: Crowell, 1973.

INDEX

OTHER TITLES FROM LERNER AND A&E®:

Arthur Ashe
Bill Gates
Bruce Lee
Carl Sagan
Chief Crazy Horse
Christopher Reeve
Eleanor Roosevelt
George Lucas
Gloria Estefan
Jack London
Jacques Cousteau
Jane Austen
Jesse Owens
Jesse Ventura
Jimi Hendrix
John Glenn
Latin Sensations
Legends of Dracula

Legends of Santa Claus
Louisa May Alcott
Madeleine Albright
Mark Twain
Maya Angelou
Mohandas Gandhi
Mother Teresa
Nelson Mandela
Princess Diana
Queen Cleopatra
Queen Latifah
Rosie O'Donnell
Saint Joan of Arc
Thurgood Marshall
Wilma Rudolph
Women in Space
Women of the Wild West

ABOUT THE AUTHOR

Tom Streissguth lives in Florida and works as a writer and editor. He has written more than twenty-five nonfiction books for young people, including biographies and books on history. His volumes in the BIOGRAPHY® series include *Legends of Dracula, Jesse Owens, Queen Cleopatra, John Glenn,* and *Jack London.* Tom has also written scripts for television.

PHOTO ACKNOWLEDGMENTS

Photographs used with permission of: North Wind Picture Archives, pp. 2, 30, 33, 62, 84, 92; Brown Brothers, pp. 6, 76, 79 (left); The Edgar Allan Poe Museum of The Poe Foundation, Inc., pp. 12, 20, 34; The Valentine Museum, Richmond, Virginia, pp. 14, 96; The Library of Virginia, p. 17; Archive Photos, pp. 19, 24, 27, 79 (right), 102, 104; Mansell Collection/TimePix, pp. 31, 42; Corbis/Bettmann, pp. 36, 44, 60, 69, 88; National Archives (NWDNS-111-V-4202), p. 46; Print Collection, Miriam and Ira D. Wallach Division of Art, Prints and Photographs, The New York Public Library, Astor, Lenox and Tilden Foundations, p. 52; The Historical Society of Pennsylvania, Society Portrait Collection, p. 58; Library of Congress, p. 67; Weidenfeld and Nicolson Archives, p. 74; American Stock/Archive Photos, p. 98.

Front and back cover photos courtesy of: Brown Brothers